WILLIAM HATFIELD

IT'S A NEW DAY

WITH ENDLESS POSSIBLITIES

WILLIAM HATFIELD

ISBN: 978-1-990362-24-8

DEDICATION

I would like to dedicate this book to all those who desire to be conformed into the image of Jesus. There is a remnant of believers who are tired of the status quo and want a more personal relationship with the Holy Spirit.

ACKNOWLEDGEMENTS

I would like to say thank you to believers everywhere who have been examples to me. The bible says we are gazing stock and should do good for each other.

Doing good to the household of faith includes giving time, talents, and treasure. Time = presence, participation, love. Showing up, listening, looking people in the eye, accepting, communicating, affirming, sharpening. These values reflect God giving time, specifically through the saints who were born again after the very image of God. Let us see the image of God manifested in our lives.

PROLOGUE

I find people who love the status quo with no change of pace boring and poor fellowship. I enjoy adventure and challenges. I have been stuck in a situation for over five years because of illness surgeries and lack of finances. My prayer at time is to be delivered from all bondages, physical, emotional, and financial. This is my journey.

CONTENTS

1.THE PAST

Had an interesting dream last night.... I was driving my old 1976 one ton I used to own for roofing and got tired so pulled into a rest stop and fell asleep. I was woken up by a female knocking on the passenger window. I unrolled the window and asked her how I could help her; she asked me to release her. I looked at her arm which was raised and stuck on the top of the box of the truck like she was reaching for something inside the box of the truck. I helped her get her hand free and asked her What she was doing. She said they were robbing farmers of their stuff and then I noticed a man trying to get into my driver's side door which was locked. She pulled a pistol and told me to get out. I started to drive away, and she shot at me and missed as I was driving away, she shot a few more times at the truck then I woke up.

Interpretation is... if I or anyone hold onto the past it will rob you (the farmer) of seeds planted and try to kill you or do you much harm. I quickly repented and released all females and males that have been in my mind that has harmed me in the past. I committed them to the Lord and asked for deliverance from the thoughts of their actions. Freedom in my soul from the past will help me harvest seeds already planted years ago. The season of harvest is upon us.

Your past may be pleasant, filled with love and kindness or just the opposite. Bottom line is we all have a yesterday. Depending upon the area of my past that suddenly pops into my mind determines the quick spark of emotion that goes with it. Emotions are a powerful thing which can make or break your day.

Each morning begins another adventure. How do you choose to start the adventure? Feeling mad, sad, glad or with a sense of excitement? I say with a sense of excitement because you finally learned to do the same thing the Apostle Paul did.

Philippians 3:12-14

New King James Version

Pressing Toward the Goal

12 Not that I have already attained, or am
already perfected; but I press on, that I may lay
hold of that for which Christ Jesus has also laid
hold of me. 13 Brethren, I do not count myself to
have apprehended; but one thing *I do,* forgetting
those things which are behind and reaching
forward to those things which are ahead, 14 I
press toward the goal for the prize of the upward
call of God in Christ Jesus.

Yesterday is gone never to be repeated so why do you want to keep the memory alive? My momma did this, my pastor did that, then my dog bit me oh the trauma how will I survive? Simple solution developing the fruit of longsuffering Galatians 5:22-23 NKJV will cause you to be free from the actions of other people and still love them regardless. Longsuffering is not putting up with sin sickness and other situations that Jesus redeemed us from at the cross by His shed blood. Longsuffering is putting up with other people's attitudes and strange personality traits. I have worked at developing this fruit in my life by fellowshipping with the Holy Spirit. I can walk in love and peace to a greater degree now than when I first became a believer in Jesus Christ.

Forgiving is essential and forgetting those things which were yesterday sets us free for exciting faith adventures of today and an overwhelming hope and joy looking forward to the next adventure. Reaching forward to those things which are ahead? What's Paul talking about?

Do you have an idea or even a small thought in your imagination of your destiny? Fellowship with the Holy Spirit will cause revelation to dawn upon your heart concerning your destiny. Once destiny is revealed you can extend your hand to reach for it and choose to walk it out in your life.

The upward call of God in Christ Jesus? Isn't that for those folks in a pulpit ministry leading the church? Not exclusively!! To many times leaders have exalted their position over lay people. When we stand at the judgment seat of Christ our

self-exalted position will not be taken into consideration. The faithfulness to what God has called you to do is what will be taken into consideration.

Here is a thought to explore, what do you find joy in doing outside of your career, job, daily duties of life? Something that you could see yourself doing if you never had to work for a living? Put away any lust of the flesh pride of life, things about laying around on a beach drinking wine and having others serve you. What could you find joy in while promoting the kingdom of Heaven?

I have found real joy in writing. I can express my feelings, revelations, knowledge, and understandings as I grow in my fellowship with the Holy Spirit. I have chosen to forget my yesterdays with all the joy and pain associated with it. There is an old saying I think of often "yesterday is gone, tomorrow never comes and today is the only constant in the time realm." How are you going to live out today?

2.START YOUR DAY WITH PEACE

To start your day with peace is a great foundation to build on. Peace is a fruit of the Spirit. Galatians 5:22-23 New King James Version

[22] But the fruit of the Spirit is love, joy, peace, longsuffering,
kindness, goodness, faithfulness, [23] gentleness, self-control. Against such there is no law.

When peace is your foundation, it will prepare you to look at the day's activities with a sense of confidence. The concept of "peace" in the Old Testament primarily refers to **wholeness, total health, total welfare**. It covers the sum total of God's blessings to a person who belongs to the covenant community. When you have peace with God you have confidence in His desire to help you overcome the adventures of the day.

1 John 5:14-15

New King James Version

Confidence and Compassion in Prayer

14 Now this is the confidence that we have in Him,
that if we ask anything according to His will, He
hears us. **15** And if we know that He hears us,
whatever we ask, we know that we have the petitions that we have asked of Him.

When we have confidence toward God and in God the realm of unlimited stands in our path.

Romans 15:13 New King James Version

13 Now may the God of hope fill you with all joy and peace in believing, that you may abound in hope by the power of the Holy Spirit.

It's your choice to let God lead, direct, and watch over you or do your own thing. Many believers forget that after they confess Jesus as lord believe He rose from the dead and receive him as savior everything doesn't become automatic. You still have choices to make besides fire insurance. Submission to Jesus as LORD.

Giving up your life and throne thereof and yielding the throne of your life to the Holy Spirit. Sometimes it's an hourly choice as we are presented with trials and temptations. Sometimes pride gets in the way, and we say, "I got this God". That's probably when you should submit most to him. God is only good and

all-knowing and all powerful. He knows the direction you should go even if it seems unreasonable to your understanding, once you start walking it out understanding comes as enlightenment or revelation.

In your relationship with the Holy Spirit try to build a habit in you to acknowledge him with thanksgiving every morning. Praise will silence negative thoughts that may try to follow you from yesterday to today. Allow the God of peace to fellowship with you instantly when you open your eyes. This is a guide I use for my life. I go to sleep at night in peace, then I know I have overcome the adventures of that day. If I am in turmoil the adventure is still alive and raging. If I am overwhelmed by the adventure, I commit it to the God of comfort the Holy Spirit and trust in Him to help me overcome the adventure. I can then rest in hope and peace knowing I can rest and not be afraid. I forget that day's activities and have hope in my mind and heart for strength when I wake up to put that adventure to rest then start the next adventure.

3.THE SWORD OF THE SPIRIT

When you mix the prophet (prophetic) with the word of faith you have the sword of the spirit in action. The sword of the spirit takes the word of God out of legalism by denominational empire to put people in bondage to freedom with joy.

The spirit of rejection is strong in this Laodicean church era.

Revelation 3:14-22

New King James Version

The Lukewarm Church

14 "And to the angel of the church of the
Laodiceans write,

'These things say the Amen, the Faithful and True
Witness, the Beginning of the creation of
God: 15 "I know your works, that you are neither
cold nor hot. I could wish you were cold or

hot. [16] So then, because you are lukewarm, and
neither cold nor hot, I will vomit you out of My
mouth. [17] Because you say, 'I am rich, have
become wealthy, and have need of nothing'—
and do not know that you are wretched,
miserable, poor, blind, and naked— [18] I counsel
you to buy from Me gold refined in the fire, that
you may be rich; and white garments, that you
may be clothed, *that* the shame of your
nakedness may not be revealed; and anoint your
eyes with eye salve, that you may see. [19] As many
as I love, I rebuke and chasten. Therefore,
be zealous and repent. [20] Behold, I stand at the
door and knock. If anyone hears My voice and
opens the door, I will come in to him and dine
with him, and he with Me. [21] To him who
overcomes I will grant to sit with Me on My
throne, as I also overcame and sat down with My
Father on His throne.

[22] "He who has an ear, let him hear what the
Spirit says to the churches."

You may attend a certain denomination which started as a revelation of God's truth as all denominations had their beginnings. Man, eventually get their hands on it and turn it into an empire that exalts its leaders and builds it according to the agenda and motivation of men while still declaring themselves as a move of God. Problem is that if you think you have a call of God on your life and present it before the leaders you will be told you are wrong. Simply because you don't fit their religious ideas or understanding. When you get rejected by pastor great (in his own mind) the temptation to take offence at the rejection is strong. Some take offence, some brush it off for what it is, an attack of Satanic forces through men to persecute the call and anointing of God on your life.

The call of God could be anything from works ministry to a five-fold ministry. Writing books could be a desire because the Spirit of God has called you to this ministry. Problem is too many people think they "know" but are actually operating in religious ignorance. God calls you and men who are building their religious empire will persecute the called because of the anointing on your life to bring people into the freedom of Christ to fellowship with the Holy Spirit. Fellowship with the Holy Spirit takes the attention away from the empire and puts it on the kingdom of God which is to build up the body of Christ and lead the lost to the saving knowledge of Jesus Christ.

FREEDOM IN CHRIST

When you in Christ have been free from the spirit of rejection you should set others free as well. The spirit of rejection can and will hide to stay in people to keep them from operating in the destiny God has for them. You can set them free by operating in the prophetic and the word of faith. I say prophetic as symbolic of the manifestations of the Holy Spirit especially the three revelation gifts. The manifestation of the Holy Spirit could be categorized in three ways.

The power gifts, the revelation gifts, the speaking gifts. A gift is not for the giver but the receiver who is in need.

God does everything in the spiritual realm first then manifests in the natural or physical realm. Ephesians 3:20-21 New King James Version

20 Now to Him who is able to do exceedingly abundantly above all that we ask or think, according to the power that works in
us, **21** to Him *be* glory in the church by Christ Jesus to all generations, forever and ever. Amen.

It's the Holy Ghost that is at work in us and fellowship with Him opens up the spiritual realm for you to be free from all bondage and you to be a vessel to set others free.

2 Corinthians 13:14

New International Version

14 May the grace of the Lord Jesus Christ, and the love of God, and the fellowship of the Holy Spirit be with you all.

All the manifestations of the Holy Spirit are important and fulfill a purpose. I personally believe the revelation gifts or manifestations are designed to give direction and enable believers to see through the eye of faith. When your spiritual eyes are open you can see the source of the problems that is keeping people confined and limited.

The revelation gifts are THE WORD OF WISDOM which is a piece not the total knowledge of future events in the life of an individual, or organizational structure Family, business, religion they may be involved with. THE WORD OF KNOWLEDGE which is again a piece not the total understanding of past and current events in the life of an individual. We as human beings are victims of action to reaction. We react to situations we have been influenced by from our past. This may be on a subconscious level so deep we miss it totally and justify it by saying that's just who I am. This brings us to the third revelation manifestation. THE DISCERNING OF

SPIRITS which is the Holy Spirit opening your eyes to see in the spiritual realm which is a different dimension than the natural realm. The spiritual realm affects the natural realm. Through the discerning of Spirits, you may see Jesus, angels, demons, or discern the heart of an individual. Their motives and purposeful agendas become revealed. The purpose of this is not to have a secret revealed to hold it over people but to help them find freedom in Christ.

1 Corinthians 12:8-11

New King James Version

8 for to one is given the word of wisdom through
the Spirit, to another the word of knowledge
through the same Spirit, 9 to another faith by the
same Spirit, to another gifts of healings by the
same Spirit, 10 to another the working of miracles,
to another prophecy, to another discerning of
spirits, to another *different* kinds of tongues, to
another the interpretation of tongues. 11 But one
and the same Spirit works all these

things, distributing to each one individually as He wills.

The Spirit of God knows the motivation of your heart. Unless the motivation of your heart is from the fruit of the spirit from Galatians 5 these manifestations may not come through you.

Galatians 5:22-23New King James
Version[22] But the fruit of the Spirit is love, joy, peace, longsuffering,
kindness, goodness, faithfulness, [23] gentleness, self-control. Against such there is no law.

I believe the fruit of the spirit is the nature of God given to us in the new birth as believers in Christ.

2 Peter 1:4

New King James Version

[4] by which have been given to us exceedingly great and precious promises, that through these you may be partakers of the divine nature, having escaped the corruption *that is* in the world through lust.

Fellowship with the Holy Spirit will open the prophetic so that the Word of God that you have stored in your heart, influenced your soul with becomes more than just pretty words on a page. The Word of God will become alive and personal influencing the course of your life and destiny.

We are born again to manifest the glory of God in and through our lives.

4.REFLECTION

The way your life is going reflects what is going on in your heart. Many if not most believers in Christ fail to make the connection that your heart and your lifestyle are connected. To separate the two is foolishness to the extreme. I have watched Christian's drink alcohol smoke marijuana and live ungodly lives and justify it by saying God knows my heart as if the two were totally distinct from each other.

In the Bible the heart is considered the seat of life or strength. Hence, it means **mind, soul, spirit, or one's entire emotional nature and understanding**.

What does the Bible say our heart is?

The Bible defines our heart across many verses, not just in one single verse. It can be easy to miss.

God created us with three parts: spirit, soul, and body. So where does our heart fit in?

The Word of God shows us that our heart isn't a fourth, separate part of our being. Instead, our heart is a composition of all three components of our soul—our **mind**, **emotion**, and **will**—plus the most important part of our spirit—
our **conscience**. Let's take a look at some key verses that reveal this.

1. Matthew 9:4

"And Jesus, knowing their thoughts, said, Why are you **thinking** evil things **in your hearts**?"

Thinking is an activity of the mind, but the Lord Jesus asked the scribes why they were thinking in their hearts. This shows that our **mind** is part of our heart.

2. Acts 11:23

"Who, when he arrived and saw the grace of God, rejoiced and encouraged them all to remain with the Lord with **purpose** of **heart**."

To *purpose* is to decide strongly to do something, which is an exercise of our will. So, this verse shows that our **will** is part of our heart.

3. John 16:22

"Therefore, you also now have sorrow; but I will see you again and your heart will rejoice, and no one takes your joy away from you."

Rejoicing is related to our emotions, but here we see that our heart rejoices. This shows us that our emotion is also part of our heart.

4. Hebrews 10:22

"Let us come forward to the Holy of Holies with a true heart in full assurance of faith, having our hearts sprinkled from an evil conscience and having our bodies washed with pure water."

Having our hearts sprinkled from an evil conscience indicates that our conscience is also part of our heart.

This is further confirmed by the phrase "if our heart blames us" in 1 John 3:20. Since our conscience blames, or condemns, us when we've done something wrong, this verse also makes it very clear that our conscience is part of our heart.

The importance of our heart

The verses above show us that our heart does much more than we might have thought. In addition to sensing the wide range of human emotions, our heart thinks, decides, and perceives right from wrong.

Now let's look at two reasons why the function of our heart is so important.

We love with our heart.

Jesus said in Mark 12:30:

"And you shall love the Lord your God from your whole heart."

If we didn't have a heart, we couldn't sense love or love in return. God created us with a heart so we could have a loving relationship with Him. So, in a very real sense, our heart is at the center of our relationship with God.

Our heart is the gateway of our being.

Besides being the center of our relationship with God, our heart is also the gateway, or doorway, of our whole being.

“Our relationship with the Lord is always begun and maintained by the heart. Of course, to contact the Lord is a matter of the spirit, but this must be initiated and maintained by the heart, for our heart is the gateway of our whole being.”

For our heart to be the gateway of our entire being means what we allow in and out is determined by our heart. For example, we can close our heart to certain people and open it to others.

“In other words, the heart becomes both the entrance and the exit of our being. Whatever enters into us must enter through the heart. Whatever comes out from us must proceed through the heart.”

When we consider our experience of salvation, this point becomes clear to us. As we heard how the Lord Jesus died on the cross for our sins, we were convicted of our sinfulness; at the same time, we began to appreciate Jesus and what He did for us. We sensed the depth and sweetness of His love for us. So, we opened the doors of our heart to believe in Him and accept Him as our Savior. At that time, we received Him in our spirit and were born again with His divine life. But it was our heart that was first touched and opened to let Him in.

Our heart and our relationship with the Lord

We were created by God in such a marvelous way! We have a spirit to contact, receive, and contain Him as life, and a heart to love Him. He wants to be our life and He wants us to love Him with our whole heart.

As we read in the first excerpt above, our relationship with the Lord is *begun* with our heart. It's also *maintained* by our heart. This is why the condition of our heart is so important.

With any relationship, when a problem arises, we need to address it. We shouldn't think the problem will go away by itself. Maybe we have a certain attitude toward the other person, or certain negative thoughts about them. Maybe we've said or done something that hurt the other person, but we're unwilling to make amends. To leave such things unresolved can only result in damaging the relationship.

In the same way, in order for us to be in harmony with the Lord and enjoy a loving relationship with Him, we need to address any problem that arises between us and the Lord. Such problems are always on *our* side and involve our heart.

In fact, many difficulties in our Christian life that prevent us from progressing are really issues in our heart—that is, in our mind, emotion, will, or conscience.

For instance, we might have a problem in our heart because our thoughts about a certain matter don't match the Lord's thoughts. Or maybe the feelings we have toward someone don't correspond with the Lord's feelings. Perhaps we insist on going our own way because our stubborn will is hardened. Or we may have a problem in our conscience because we haven't dealt with things that have offended and displeased the Lord. With our heart in such a state, how can our relationship with the Lord be sweet and harmonious?

Now we can see how important it is to be aware of the condition of our heart in order to maintain our loving and warm relationship with the Lord. When a problem arises between us and the Lord, we can simply turn our heart to Him and pray, "Lord Jesus, I open my heart to You. I don't want anything to come between You and me. I love You, Lord."

5.ANCIENT OF DAYS

JESUS CHRIST IS THE ANCIENT OF DAYS

Enoch is the subject of many Jewish and Christian traditions. He was considered the author of the Book of Enoch and also called the scribe of judgment. In the New Testament, Enoch is referenced in **the Gospel of Luke, the Epistle to**

the Hebrews, and in the Epistle of Jude, the last of which also quotes from it. Even though it is not canon of scripture it has been referred to in the new testament.

Daniel 7:9

"I kept looking.

Until thrones were set up,

And the Ancient of Days took His seat.

His vesture was like white snow.

And the hair of His head like pure wool.

His throne was ablaze with flames,

Its wheels were a burning fire.

Daniel 7:13

"I kept looking in the night visions,

And behold, with the clouds of heaven

One like a Son of Man was coming,

And He came up to the Ancient of Days

And was presented before Him.

Most believers don't recognize Jesus as the ancient of days but as the Son of God or the Son of man. The previous verse seems to make a distinction. The Son of Man presenting himself before the Ancient of Days.

Daniel 7:22

until the Ancient of Days came and judgment was passed in favor of the saints of the Highest One, and the time arrived when the saints took possession of the kingdom.

Psalm 90:2

Before the mountains were born

Or You gave birth to the earth and the world,

Even from everlasting to everlasting, You are

God.

Isaiah 44:6

"Thus says the Lord, the King of Israel and his Redeemer, the Lord of hosts:

'I am the first and I am the last,

And there is no God besides Me.

Revelation 1:14-15

His head and His hair were white like white wool, like snow; and His eyes were like a flame of fire. His feet were like burnished bronze, when it has been made to glow in a furnace, and His voice was like the sound of many waters.

The ancient of days was portrayed as an old man with white hair and He was one God, and everyone bowed before him. I believe this was through tradition and lack of revelation of the trinity. Portrayed as an old man helped the natural mind cope with an eternal God was never had a beginning or an end.

Jesus declaring, he was the I am, and the Word of God simply freaked out the tradition holders such as pharisees, Sadducees, lawyers and others that held to information that was handed down from previous generations.

John 8: 56 Your father Abraham rejoiced that he
would see my day. He saw it and was glad." 57 So
the Jews said to him, "You are not yet fifty years
old, and have you seen Abraham?" 58 Jesus said
to them, "Truly, truly, I say to you, before
Abraham was, I am." 59 So they picked up stones
to throw at him, but Jesus hid himself and went
out of the temple.

John 1 New King James Version

The Eternal Word

1 In the beginning was the Word, and the Word
was with God, and the Word was God. **2** He was in

the beginning with God. 3 All things were made through Him, and without Him nothing was made that was made. 4 In Him was life, and the life was the light of men. 5 And the light shines in the darkness, and the darkness did not comprehend it.

The ancient of days is not singular but triune as the bible says in genesis 1:26. We can then identify God the Father, God the Son, and God the Holy Spirit the triune being as THE ANCIENT OF DAYS.

Where is the Ancient of Days residing now?

1 Peter 1:23
having been born again, not of corruptible seed but incorruptible, through the word of God which lives and abides forever,

Luke 8:11
Now this is the meaning of the parable: The seed is the word of God.

John 1:13

children born not of blood, nor of the desire or will of man, but born of God.

We as believers in Christ have been born again of THE ANCIENT OF DAYS and He resides in us.

1 Corinthians 6:19

New King James Version

[19] Or do you not know that your body is the temple of the Holy Spirit *who is* in you, whom you have from God, and you are not your own?

So here is my point of bringing up the Ancient of Days. Don't see the triune God as an old out of date being, but a timeless individual that now resides within you. When we got born again not only did the Ancient of Days come into our body, but we were baptized into His body as well.

1 Corinthians 12:12-27

New King James Version

Unity and Diversity in One Body

12 For as the body is one and has many members, but all the members of that one body, being many, are one body, so also *is* Christ. 13 For by one Spirit we were all baptized into one body—whether Jews or Greeks, whether slaves or free—and have all been made to drink into one Spirit. 14 For in fact the body is not one member but many.

15 If the foot should say, "Because I am not a hand, I am not of the body," is it therefore not of the body? 16 And if the ear should say, "Because I am not an eye, I am not of the body," is it therefore not of the body? 17 If the whole body *were* an eye, where *would be* the hearing? If the whole *were* hearing, where *would be* the smelling? 18 But now God has set the members, each one of them, in the body just as He pleased. 19 And if they were all one member, where *would* the body *be?*

20 But now indeed *there are* many members, yet one body. 21 And the eye cannot say to the hand,

"I have no need of you"; nor again the head to
the feet, "I have no need of you." 22 No, much
rather, those members of the body which seem
to be weaker are necessary. 23 And
those *members* of the body which we think to be
less honorable, on these we bestow greater
honor; and our unpresentable *parts* have greater
modesty, 24 but our presentable *parts* have no
need. But God composed the body, having given
greater honor to that *part* which lacks it, 25 that
there should be no schism in the body,
but *that* the members should have the same care
for one another. 26 And if one member suffers, all
the members suffer with *it;* or if one member is
honored, all the members rejoice with *it.*

27 Now you are the body of Christ, and members
individually.

He in us and us in Him then we are all partakers of the divine nature of the Ancient of Days.

2 Peter 1:4

New King James Version

4 by which have been given to us exceedingly
great and precious promises, that through these
you may be partakers of the divine nature, having
escaped the corruption *that is* in the world
through lust.

Then being partakers of the divine nature and God doesn't have love but is love; **1 John 4:7-11 New King James Version**

Knowing God Through Love

7 Beloved, let us love one another, for love is of
God; and everyone who loves is born of God and
knows God. 8 He who does not love does not
know God, for God is love. 9 In this the love of
God was manifested toward us, that God has
sent His only begotten Son into the world, that
we might live through Him. 10 In this is love, not
that we loved God, but that He loved us and sent
His Son *to be* the propitiation for our
sins. 11 Beloved, if God so loved us, we also ought
to love one another.

Our conduct doesn't determine the love God has for us. No matter how good we perform or our failure to perform the works we hold so honorable in our thoughts God's love for us doesn't change. The Ancient of Days lives in us and we live in The Ancient of Days and His love is never changing why do we allow our days to be manipulated by lower natures and changing circumstances? The reason is we rely too much on information which comes from the tree of knowledge. **Genesis 2:17 New King James Version**

17 but of the tree of the knowledge of good and evil you shall not eat, for in the day that you eat of it you shall surely die."

When we receive revelation which is higher than information our days will become limitless. **Ephesians 1:17-19 New King James Version**

17 that the God of our Lord Jesus Christ, the Father of glory, may give to you the spirit of wisdom and revelation in the knowledge of

Him, [18] the eyes of your understanding being enlightened; that you may know what is the hope of His calling, what are the riches of the glory of His inheritance in the saints, [19] and what *is* the exceeding greatness of His power toward us who believe, according to the working of His mighty power.

Through revelation of The Ancient of Days living in us and we in him our days can become limitless and joyful.

6.WONDER

When in wonder what do I do? When in wonder where do I go? When in wonder what do I say? Interesting questions that go through a lot of people's minds. I too have wonder; to make me question life and how it works itself out in my daily activities.

won·der /ˈwəndər/

noun

noun: **wonder**

a feeling of surprise mingled with admiration, caused by something beautiful, unexpected, unfamiliar, or inexplicable.

"he had stood in front of it, observing the intricacy of the ironwork with the wonder of a child"

Similar: awe admiration wonderment fascination

surprise astonishment Amazement

+the quality of a person or thing that causes wonder.

plural noun: **wonders**

"Athens was a place of wonder and beauty"

Similar: marvel miracle phenomenon wonderful thing

Sensation sight spectacle beauty curiosity rarity nonpareil

a strange or remarkable person, thing, or event.

"the electric trolley car was looked upon as the wonder of the age"

having remarkable properties or abilities.

modifier noun: **wonder** "a wonder drug" a surprising event or situation.

"it is a wonder that losses are not much greater"

verb

verb: **wonder**; 3rd person present: **wonders**; past tense: **wondered**; past participle: **wondered**; gerund or present participle: **wondering**

1. desire or be curious to know something.

"how many times have I written that; I wonder?"

Similar: ponder ask oneself think about meditate on

reflect on deliberate about muse on speculate about

conjecture puzzle about be curious about be inquisitive about

cudgel one's brains about used to express a polite question or request.

"I wonder whether you have thought more about it?"

2. feel doubt. "I **wonder about** such a marriage."
3. feel admiration and amazement, marvel.

"people stood by and **wondered at** such bravery"

Similar: marvel be amazed be filled with amazement

be filled with admiration be astonished be surprised

be awed stand in awe be full of wonder be lost for words

not believe one's eyes/ears do not know what to say be dumbfounded

gape goggle gawk be flabbergasted boggle be surprised.

"if I feel compassion for her, it is not to be **wondered at**"

Similar: be surprised express surprise find it surprising

be astonished/amazed.

Lots of meanings to the word wonder. Not surprised that we experience many of them each day, from waking up in the morning thinking about days activities to be amazed by surprising events that cause joy to flood our souls.

Living in a dark, pessimistic world where Satan is the god of this world system and believers in Christ are going against the flow; may cause a believer to think a wonder that causes joy may be a sign the God of heaven is at work in your life. This very well may be true as the Holy Spirit does work through signs and wonders. **2 Corinthians 12:12** - Truly the signs of an apostle were wrought among you in all patience, in signs, and wonders, and mighty deeds.

Isaiah 8:18 - Behold, I and the children whom the LORD hath given me [are] for signs and for wonders in Israel from the LORD of hosts, which dwelleth in mount Zion.

Signs and wonders can be exciting and enticing to follow the person they came through, but Jesus warned us not to do this.

John 4:48 New King James Version

Then Jesus said to him, "Unless you *people* see signs and wonders, you will by no means believe."

Amplified Bible

Then Jesus said to him, "Unless you [people] see [miraculous] signs and wonders, you [simply] will not believe."

Acts 2:19

I will show wonders in the heavens above and signs on the earth below, blood and fire and billows of smoke.

Acts 2:22

Men of Israel, listen to this message: Jesus of Nazareth was a man certified by God to you by miracles, wonders, and signs, which God did among you through Him, as you yourselves know.

People have tendency to be amazed at signs, wonders and things that fall outside their natural reasoning abilities and when they see them they want to follow the person they came through. Not all but many people that produce signs and wonders do not have the kingdom of God as their priority but themselves and financial status.

Mark 13:22

For false Christs and false prophets will appear and perform signs and wonders that would deceive even the elect, if that were possible.

Fellowship with the Holy Spirit will save you from religious con men who amaze your soul through spectacular events. When you are in constant fellowship with the Holy Spirit you will not have to wonder about each day but know the goodness of God will manifest each day.

Psalm 23:6 New King James Version

6 Surely goodness and mercy shall follow me
All the days of my life;
And I will dwell in the house of the LORD
Forever.

An interesting thought to meditate on. Through your fellowship with the Holy Spirit signs and wonders manifest in and through your life to others as a testimony of the goodness of God in your life. Mark 9:23 New King James Version

23 Jesus said to him, "If you can believe, all things *are* possible to him who believes."

A wonder people fail to realize yet and living out is, words determine the course of your life. The words you speak and choose to believe from others will affect the course and direction of your life.

7.CHANGE YOUR MIND AND WORDS SPOKEN

Most people whether they are born again or not fail to realize how words believed and spoken impact their lives. Words spoken by others over your life if you choose to believe them can cause you to go in a direction you may not find enjoyable.

Luke 6:45 New King James Version

45 A good man out of the good treasure of his heart brings forth good; and an evil man out of the evil treasure of his heart brings forth evil. For out of the abundance of the heart his mouth speaks.

You have heard the saying, “You will eat your words.” That phrase stems from the book of Proverbs – chapter 18. Verse 20 and 21 say this,

From the fruit of their mouth a person’s stomach

is filled; with the harvest of their lips, they are satisfied. The tongue has the power of life and death, and those who love it will eat its fruit.

Words have the power of life and death. The way you use them will have a profound impact on the climate of your life.

5 Suggestions for Using Your Words Wisely

Words can define the culture and tone of your family, business, etc. – Do you affirm the behavior that you want to see more of? Do you praise your kids? Does your wife know how beautiful she is to you? Or do you criticize and tear down? The words you use will absolutely set the tone of your business or family. Don't be the guy who complains all the time and wonders why his company has a negative culture.

Gossip is a cancer – Gossip ruins culture. It is a sign of cowardice. It disrespects everyone involved. Don't allow it – period.

Beware of joking and teasing – This is a sensitive subject for me as I have wounded many people by what I believed was innocent teasing. Teasing destroys trust and breaks down communication. It can strike at the insecurities of a person's heart. I grew up pretending like teasing didn't bother me. It did. As a result, I kept everyone at a distance. This wound impacted my relationship with my friends, my parents, and even my marriage. It is something I've had to work through. Be very careful with innocent teasing.

Be intentional with your words – Some of us are naturally very thoughtful with our words. Some of us are not. I encourage you to understand the truth that King Solomon wrote about in the proverb above. Words have the power of life and death. Think about the good you can do with your words. If you don't, your words will control you. And you will reap what you sow. Use your words to bless and encourage. Speak the truth in love.

Silence – This is my challenge to you. Build times of silence into your day. We are bombarded with so much noise all day long that it is difficult to think. "The person who doesn't know how to be silent doesn't know how to speak." Those in my life that give life with their words are thoughtful. They have these times in their day when they are silent. Try it.

8.OVERRIDING POWER OF JOY

Joy a fruit of the spirt has power to destroy bondages such as grief, sorrow, sadness, and anything the enemy Satan can throw at you. Satan a creature of pride hates to be laughed at.

What If We Became Friends? Would there be continued joy in the friendship? Would encouraging and blessing each other in the motive of love be the goal?

I found this piece on the internet and thought it was valuable

The Power of Joy

By Thomas N. Hopper

What is joy? In our process of maturing, we often think that joy is the result of happy circumstances. And it may be. I have seen a little rabbit run across the sidewalk and into the grass, and I had a feeling of joy.

We find joy in happy experiences and in our relationships with our loved ones. But joy is a deeper thing than just the result of happy circumstances. If it were only such a result, there would be times, many times, when we could not have joy; and in Truth, joy is always ours.

A more mature view of joy is that it is a by-product of serving others, of sharing good.

It may be the sense of a job well and honestly done. But joy is even more than this. It is not a result of anything—of good deeds, of doing work well, of anything else. Joy is not a result; it is a cause. It can happen to us, but we can also make it happen and make other things happen because of it.

Joy is a spiritual principle that we can lay hold of and use. It is a principle that we can use all the time, whether outer conditions are as favorable as we would like them to be or not. And if they are not what we wish, we can do more than put up with them; we can make them improve by using the principle of spiritual joy.

Joy is a good influence in any situation, and there are many ways we can express joy—with positive thoughts, pleasant words, a smile, even by using our sense of humor. ...

As Nehemiah said, "The joy of the Lord is your strength" (Neh. 8:10), because joy in our inward being irresistibly calls forth joy in the outer world.

... We cannot wait for circumstances to bring us joy; we must make our own joy and let it act upon circumstances.

One of the paradoxes of Truth is that a happy heart draws to itself all that it needs for happiness. And we can keep our hearts happy by drawing on the wellspring of joy that is a part of our spiritual nature.

Any problem or trouble can be overcome by the power of joy. Some overcoming's take longer than others. But even if we are dealing with a problem of long standing, that is no reason to despair or to give up hope of solving new problems that come along.

But how do we cultivate joy in the heart, more joy in our lives?

Use is the law of increase. If we want more joy, we must use joy. We must lay hold on joy and let it well up from within us through thought, word, and action.

First, we must realize that God is the source of our joy, the only Source. People and things and situations are wonderful when all is well, but since they may change, we must not place our spiritual dependence on them. We must depend on the Source which cannot change and from which all good flows.

Second, we must be poised and centered in the Christ mind to use the power of joy. We can make our work and play alike, pleasant, and creative, if we practice the presence of God. When we realize that we are always one with God, we work with the joy and ease of the power of God within us. Even when our attention is on the work at hand, we can learn to go through every day with the feeling of God's presence, with the knowledge of God's love, power, and joy flowing through us.

Third, being centered in the Christ mind, we can speak the word and do that which is needed to bring forth joy. Remember: ... But suppose we cannot feel any joy in our being? Are there ways we can make it spring up? Indeed, there are! There are material ways, such as cheering ourselves up with bright clothes, a bouquet of flowers, a good dinner, or some other pleasant experience.

We should also, however, use the spiritual ways of cultivating joy. We can stop turning our attention so far inward on our own personal universe and its problems. We can turn outward instead, to consider others and what we can do for them. When we can bring joy to others, we always find joy ourselves. ...

Another way we can increase in our hearts is by counting our blessings and giving thanks for them.

We do not need a great stimulus to feel the joy of giving thanks. If we appreciate the smallest blessing that comes to us or that has always been with us, and take nothing for granted, we find that we are living in a constant state of joy.

There are three chief things to remember about joy if we want its power to live by. It is the cause, not the effect, of good in our lives. It increases for us through use, because when we speak, think, and act with joy, there is no room for anything else in our lives. We can cultivate joy with material helps and by serving others, turning our attention outward rather than inward, and giving sincere thanks to God for all our blessings.

When I focus on myself and some of the hardships, I had to endure joy doesn't seem to fit in the equation. Your focus can quickly turn to sadness and depression. I had a revelation of helping others within the sphere of my influence to the best of my abilities, and when I do, focused is changed and joy rests in my soul. So if I continually practice helping others the joy will eventually change my personal circumstances to be exciting, joyful, peaceful, giving hope again rather than hopelessness and depression.

The Power of Joy is the roadmap for action takers who want real change.

For God to step in, joy and rejoicing is a fundamental requirement.

9.FAITH IN THE FUTURE BRINGS POWER IN THE PRESENT

When I say faith in the future, I am not referring to the carnal desire humans have of fame, fortune, and grandeur.

I am referring to the Holy Spirit and your personal intimate relationship. John 16:13-15

New King James Version

13 However, when He, the Spirit of truth, has come, He will guide you into all truth; for He will not speak on His own authority, but whatever He hears He will speak; and He will tell you things to come. 14 He will glorify Me, for He will take of what is Mine and declare it to you. 15 All things that the Father has are Mine. Therefore, I said that He will take of Mine and declare it to you.

You may be in a hopeless-looking situation and desire a new life complete with an abundance of finances. New occupation or even an occupation that satisfies your soul. The definition of new life could include a spouse to alleviate loneliness and have a helper to enjoy life together. You dream and desire and pray for the Holy Spirit to change everything in your current situation.

You try not to doubt and make contrary confessions, but all looks hopeless.

Regardless of how it looks, remember two things.

1. Jesus has compassion on you.

2. He will guide you through the hopelessness of your situation.

Remember the Holy Spirit knows your destiny and your current situation has not taken God by surprise. You may have been set on the sidelines for further training to walk in fellowship and obedience to the Holy Spirit. Don't yield to self-pity or depression knowing the impressions, dreams and prophetic words shall all be fulfilled in the fullness of time.

Psalm 9:1

New King James Version

9 I will praise You, O Lord, with my whole heart;

I will tell of all Your marvelous works.

Psalm 23:3

New King James Version

3 He restores my soul;

He leads me in the paths of righteousness.

For His name's sake.

The trinity knows how to bring you into the fullness of the destiny they have for your life. You may have been given a glimpse of it in dreams or visions, but if you stay steadfast and expect everything will run the course you are put on and you will walk in the dreams visions and things spoken over you by prophets of God. You will stand tall, true, and available for the Spirit of God to manifest His goodness to you and through you to others.

God's goodness to you and through you will take all limits off your life and cause you to do things in the here and now you never dreamed possible.

10.WHOSE OPINION TAKES PRIORITY?

In our generation and probably past generations people tend to think their opinion is important and feel the right to express it regardless of the impact they might have on others. The deception of fame and proclaiming your own fame deludes you into thinking others exalt you as much as you exalt yourself and think your opinion is almost deified and infallible.

When you share your calling with people you are opening yourself to their opinions and may have subjected yourself to a spirit of religion manifesting through them. You have to decide who has the better point of view? The Holy Spirit who has called you and created the gifts you have as part of your nature, or the man subjected to religious philosophies of their denominational empire. The disciples had to make a choice about who was more important.

Acts 5:29 New King James Version

29 But Peter and the other apostles answered and said: “We ought to obey God rather than men.

If you have been called by man chances are your limitations will soon become obvious because man has limits on his thinking and abilities to see tomorrow. Humans have better hindsight than foresight.

Fellowship with the Holy Spirit will take limits off of you. I will say that statement over and over until you get it fellowship with the Holy Spirit is the priority in life.

I walked in fellowship with the Holy Spirit when I was in Saskatoon Saskatchewan and still do today. The Holy Spirit lead me and a few others to start a bible study and it grew very quickly and when the church I attended heard of it they were threatened and demanded I shut it down because that’s how they started their church was in a home bible study. Pastors and leaders of churches (not all but many) get threatened when God calls someone or starts to move outside their realm of influence because they have taken control of the move of God where they got their start and can't see God doing something out side their belief structure. I was declared by the pastor of using witchcraft to draw people to the bible study. Don't allow opinions, no matter who in authority, to influence your relationship with the Holy Spirit.

Allow the fruit of the spirit or should I say develop the fruit in your life and the opinions of naysayers will be a noise easily forgotten.

Denominational empire builders will make their religious declarations and if necessary use pressure tactics to make their movement look like God is the source of their anointing and movement. When pressure is felt or in manifestation know the enemy is looking to put limitations on your life.

11. HOW CLOSE TO THE END ARE WE?

Social media is going wild with everyone's opinions concerning the end times. Earthquakes, famines, draughts, rivers, lakes drying up makes Matthew 24 a living reality. People use these events to declare we are at the end of the end times which I believe started with birth of Jesus in the earth. It was the beginning of the end for the god of this world Satan. I agree we could be living in the final hours of the end times.

The pre-tribulation rapture folks are making a lot of statements and YouTube videos as well as on other social media platforms that all the stuff happening is a signpost to the rapture of the saints. There are no signs concerning rapture. Paul, who penned the books of Thessalonians made the statement we who are alive shall be caught up with them who are asleep in Christ to meet Christ in the clouds. Read the books of Thessalonians for verification.

My personal belief is the rapture or resurrection of the church could happen at any time in history only God the Father knows the time. We as believers in Christ are to live our lives like we could be caught up instantly and yet in the same breath continue to be a witness to others every day of our lives like we will live out our lives on this earth.

God's plan has always been to bring His kingdom into the earth through mature sons who glorify Him. His initial blessing upon mankind was to release and enable them to be fruitful and multiply; fill the earth and subdue it; and have dominion over every living thing that moves on the earth (Genesis 1:28).

Visitation speaks of events and seasons. Habitation speaks of a lifestyle of overcoming faith. Visitation may be experienced by being in the right place (geographically and/or spiritually) at the right time. Habitation becomes an experiential reality for us as we are rightly placed in His body, and then discipled by guardians and stewards who are charged with our upbringing. The guardians are those of like fellowship who are encouragers to fellowship with the Holy Spirit rather than make denominal empires our priority.

It is wonderful to have a visitation of God. Emotional highs and tingly feelings may be a healing, or a miracle comes in manifestation. In the process of time the visitation is downgraded into a memory of the good old days when.

To have habitation is to have the Holy Spirit live and fellowship with you permanently. You bare His home or temple and live with you permanently never to be grieved or offended by the lusts of your flesh. Like I said before fellowship with the Holy Spirit and development of the fruit of the Spirit in your life is vital to fulfilling your destiny in Christ and live a limitless life. Let the end times take care of themselves simply because it's beyond your ability to influence or affect the timing and outcome of those events.

While you are alive on planet earth let your fellowship with the Holy Spirit be a witness to all within the sphere of your influence. The witness of a loving God who desires to be in fellowship with humanity and through that fellowship experience the goodness of God and be unlimited in your life's circumstances and abilities.

EPILOGUE

We go through life dealing with information gathered through our five physical senses thus limiting us in our realm of influence. Fellowship with the Holy Spirit will cause revelation to surpass information thus taking limitations off your soul. You choose your lifestyle and be prepared for the results. I choose fellowship with the Holy Spirit.

ABOUT THE AUTHOR

William is a kind considerate compassionate person who loves people and honors God. His desire is to fellowship with the Holy Spirit and walk according to the promptings of the Holy Spirit. He enjoys encouraging people to seek after fellowship with the trinity and experience the goodness of God.

www.ingramcontent.com/pod-product-compliance
Lightning Source LLC
LaVergne TN
LVHW010459160826
845677LV00012B/2565

* 9 7 8 1 9 9 0 3 6 2 2 4 8 *